Sabine Lohf

Making Things for Easter

Bunny Billy and Snowman Willy

You will need:

2 white and 2 brown eggs (or 4 white eggs), 1 package of varied-colored clay, 2 wooden sticks, crepe paper, clear tape, a flowerpot with soil, 1 felt-tipped marker

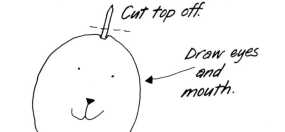

Cut top off.

Draw eyes and mouth.

1. Blow out the eggs and wash them thoroughly. (To blow out an egg, make a pinhole in one end of the egg and a larger hole [⅛ in.] in the other end. Hold the egg over a bowl and blow into the pinhole.)

Wind tape around the stick right under the bottom egg (the "body") so that the eggs cannot slide off.

2. Carefully push the eggs onto the stick and push the stick into the soil in the flowerpot.

3. Make arms and ears out of clay. Stick ears and arms on the eggs. If the clay won't stick to the eggs, use some glue.

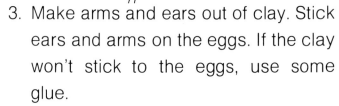

Something is still missing.

The snowman needs a nose, a hat, and arms. Make them from clay.

Use crepe paper to make scarves for the bunny and the snowman.

Find a small egg for the bunny to hold in his arms. The snowman might hold a small branch.

You can make some grass from shredded crepe paper to put around them.

Stuffed Rooster

You will need:

1 large cardboard egg that can open (they are easy to find at Eastertime), cardboard, colored construction paper, crepe paper, 1 cardboard tube from a toilet-paper roll, feathers, glue, scissors, candy eggs for filling

1. Cut a rooster head and neck from cardboard.

2. Make a 1-inch cut at the bottom of the neck, bend one half back and the other forward.

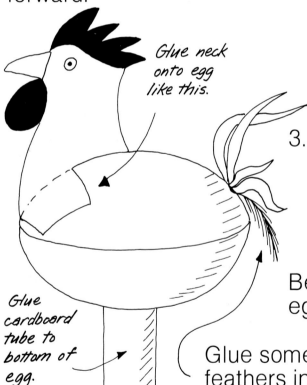

Glue neck onto egg like this.

Bend forward.

Bend back.

3. Tear up some colored construction paper to resemble feathers and glue the feathers to the back top of the egg.

Be careful not to glue the egg shut.

Glue cardboard tube to bottom of egg.

Glue some real feathers into the paper tail.

I'll give this to my best friend.

Fill the finished rooster with Easter candy or some other surprise.

Dancing Bunny

You will need:

Blown-out eggs, brown wrapping paper, felt-tip marker, glue, string

1. Cut out ears, arms, and legs from brown wrapping paper.

Arms

Legs

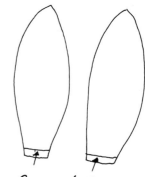

Ears

Crease bottoms.

2. Knot a long string and pass it through the holes of two blown eggs so that the knot is on the bottom of the eggs.

3. Draw a face on the top egg with a felt-tip marker.

4. Glue on the ears, arms, and legs. Use some string for whiskers.

Now dance!

If you hang the bunny on a tree branch, the breeze will make it dance.

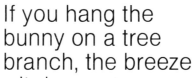

A Branch to Chase Winter Away

You will need:

1 branch (birch or forsythia), blown-out eggs, paints, brush, wooden sticks, corks, matchsticks, red ribbons and bows, red string

1. Paint the eggs red. Push a small stick through the egg and push the end of the stick into a cork. This will make it easier to paint the egg. Leave the egg on the cork to dry.

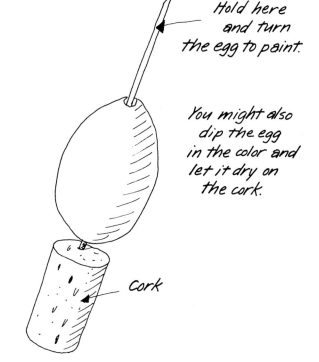

Hold here and turn the egg to paint.

You might also dip the egg in the color and let it dry on the cork.

Cork

In earlier times, it was customary for people to drive winter away by coloring eggs red and tying them to a branch. The branch was decorated with red ribbons and bows. Then the branch was paraded around the town.

2. Decorate the branch with red ribbons.

Hang the egg with red string.

This is how to put the string hanger on the egg:

Bye, bye, winter!

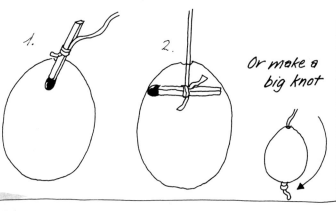

1.   2.   Or make a big knot

Paper Candy Baskets

<u>You will need:</u>
Colored construction paper, scissors, 2 brass paper fasteners

1. Cut a rectangle about 9 by 10 inches.

2. Cut on the black lines.

3. Fold on the dotted lines to form a basket.

Handle

4. Attach the handle on each side with the paper fasteners. First push the fastener through the handle. Then push it through the three other layers of paper at the end of the basket to make it secure.

Fill the basket with Easter grass and Easter candy.

Fred and Phil Decorate Easter Eggs

You will need:

Hard-boiled or blown-out eggs, cardboard, glue, scissors, paints, paintbrushes

To make Fred and Phil, it's best to use hard-boiled eggs.

Cut head, arms, and legs from cardboard.

Glue all body parts onto egg. Bend the legs so that the rabbits can stand.

Paint the face on the head.

Bend here.

Bend here.

Now we've got to paint this bunny.

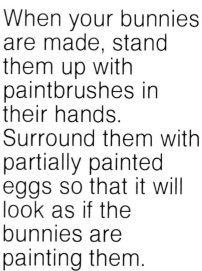

When your bunnies are made, stand them up with paintbrushes in their hands. Surround them with partially painted eggs so that it will look as if the bunnies are painting them.

If you like, they can stand in a meadow.

The Surprise Egg

 ?

You will need:

Several balloons, colored tissue paper, a knife, papier-mâché mix, plastic bowl, paints, brushes, and a surprise

1. Mix the papier-mâché paste in a bowl. (Follow the directions on the package.)

Stir, let it stand 10 minutes, then stir again, thoroughly.

2. Blow up the balloons. Make the first one big and each one after that a little smaller than the one before. They will have to fit into one another later on.

3. Stick tissue paper on each of the balloons. Use papier-mâché paste mixture and several layers of the paper. Use a different color for each balloon.

4. Let the balloons dry for two days.

5. Cut each balloon into two equal halves. (CAUTION: Be careful when using a knife. Or have an adult do the cutting for you.)

6. Nest the eggs, one inside the other, till you have one big egg with the others inside. Before stacking the eggs, paint each with a face. Hide a surprise in the smallest egg.

I wonder what's in there!

If you leave the eggs outside your bedroom door overnight, someone may put a surprise in the smallest egg for you.

18

Easter Customs

At Eastertime winter is over. Easter is always the Sunday after the first full moon of spring.

The Easter bunny and the Easter egg are very important in the celebration of Easter. In many countries the egg is the symbol of new life.

In many places eggs are dyed red before Easter. On Easter morning families and friends exchange the eggs along with a kiss and wishes for a happy Easter.

Palm Sunday is the Sunday before Easter. In many countries, people make palm bushes.

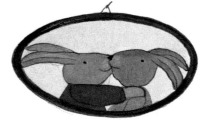

Palm bushes are made of pussy-willow and evergreen branches tied together. In Germany they are taken to church.

Wonderful breads are baked for Easter. They are made into shapes like lambs, braids, or a man holding an egg.

In some countries people set small floating candles in water to symbolize the end of winter. The candles mean that artificial lights won't be needed anymore.

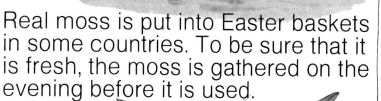

There is one myth that says that hidden treasures are visible only on Easter day.

Real moss is put into Easter baskets in some countries. To be sure that it is fresh, the moss is gathered on the evening before it is used.

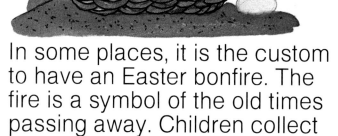

In some places, it is the custom to have an Easter bonfire. The fire is a symbol of the old times passing away. Children collect wood, straw, and even old Christmas trees for the fire.

In the old days girls would get up at sunrise and fetch water from a stream. They were not supposed to speak to anyone. A swallow of the water would bring beauty and good health.

The Easter bunny is the symbol of fertility.

A Baked Bunny

You will need:

4¼ cups flour, 1 package dry yeast, 2 tablespoons oil, salt, 1 tablespoon sugar, 1 cup lukewarm milk, marzipan paste, a large bowl, and some round, colored candies, such as jelly beans

1. Follow the directions on the package to activate the yeast.

2. Mix flour, sugar, yeast, and a pinch of salt in a large bowl.

3. Fold in oil and milk and knead till smooth.

4. Continue kneading dough on floured board.

5. Make these shapes for each of the rabbits.

Head Ears Arms Nose Body

6. Put your bunny together on a greased baking sheet. Cover with a towel and let stand one hour.

7. Bake at 425° for 15 to 20 minutes.

Make whiskers out of straw or whatever you have that would make good whiskers.

Shape a painter's palette out of marzipan paste.

Use round candies for the colors on the palette.

Set the baked bunny in a nest.

Flying Bunnies

You will need:

Balloons, blown-out eggs, needle and white thread, cardboard tube from a toilet-paper roll, white paper, colored paper, scissors, glue

Knot threads inside tube.

1. Cut the cardboard tube in half and decorate it by gluing on colored strips of paper.

2. With the needle, pull thread through in four places, spacing them evenly around the tube.

3. Glue one egg onto each tube half.

Cut and glue paper ears and arms for your bunnies.

Blow up as many balloons as you need to make each bunny fly.

Tie each of the strings to the balloon.

Let the bunnies fly from a high place, or fly them in your yard.

Hang some of these flying bunnies in your own room.

Eggshell Boats

You will need:

Several eggshell halves, clay, toothpicks, colored construction paper, glue

1. Wash out eggshells and let them dry.

2. Put some glue in the center of the eggshell. Stick some clay on the glue.

3. Cut triangles out of the paper.

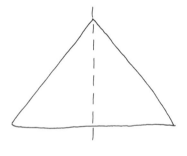

Glue a toothpick into the center of each triangle. Fold the paper in half and glue the halves together.

Push the toothpick into the clay, and your boat is done!

Float the boats in a puddle of water or in the bathtub.

Your boats will float nicely when a breeze pushes them.

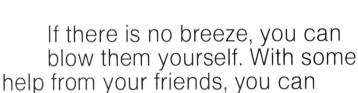

If there is no breeze, you can blow them yourself. With some help from your friends, you can create good wind power!

Who can blow a boat across the water first?

Heddy Hen and Bobby Bunny

You will need:

Yellow and brown yarn, orange and brown felt, cotton batting, 2 black beads, 2 white shirt buttons, a large needle, thread, scissors, white yarn or string

Heddy Hen

1. Make a ball of cotton batting and wind yellow yarn around the ball. Make one ball for the head and one for the body.

2. Sew the head and the body together.

3. Cut a beak, wings, feet, and comb out of orange felt.

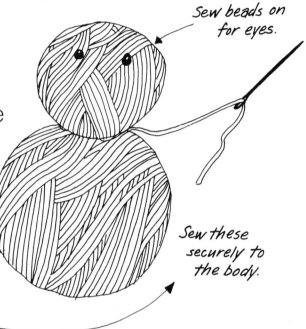

Sew beads on for eyes.

Sew these securely to the body.

I love to cuddle Heddy.

Bobby Bunny

1. Make the body exactly as you made Heddy's body.

2. Now you need five small yarn balls for the feet and a nose.

3. Cut ears out of brown felt.

4. Sew all the parts together.

5. Sew on white buttons for eyes.

6. Make whiskers from white yarn or string.

Swimming Duck

This duck can be made out of plywood or heavy cardboard. If it is made out of wood, it will last longer.

You will need:

Thin plywood (12" x 16"), saw, enamel paints, brushes, pencil, string, 1 small rock

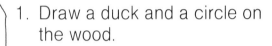

1. Draw a duck and a circle on the wood.

2. Cut out the duck and the circle with the saw. (CAUTION: Be careful when using a saw. Or have an adult do the sawing for you.) Cut a rectangle from the center of the circle, just large enough for the foot of the duck to fit through.

3. Paint the duck and the circle.

4. Tie a string to the foot of the duck where the hole is. Tie the other end of the string to a rock for an anchor. Now the duck will be able to float alone, even when the water has waves.

1, 2, 3, Make Something From an Egg for Me!

You will need:

Blown-out eggs, cotton batting, feather, colored paper, cardboard tubes from toilet-paper rolls, scissors, glue, wire, scraps of cloth, felt-tip markers

Mouse

Cut ears and a small circle for a pointy nose. Glue them on an egg.

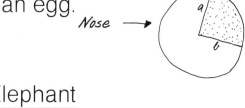

Ears

Nose →

Cut away the dotted area. Glue edges A and B together.

Ears

Trunk

Tusks

Elephant

Cut out ears, trunk, and tusks. Glue them onto another egg.

Bunny

Give him two long ears and whiskers.

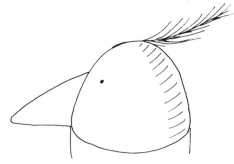

I made a princess. Her name is Amelia.

Bird

Glue a real feather on his head. Give him a red paper beak.

Grandfather

Make him a long beard out of cotton batting. Bend some wire into glasses.

Glue all the egg figures onto cardboard tubes that have been cut in half. Make faces with the markers.

Think of other figures that you can make: chickens, people, wild animals.

Dyeing, Painting, and Decorating Eggs

Eggs can be colored in different ways.

If you dye the eggs with brown onion skin, the shells will turn brown.

Spinach and thistle leaves turn eggshells green.

Beets turn the shells red.

And this is how to dye eggs with vegetables.

Boil the vegetables you are using to dye the eggs. Simmer the eggs with the vegetables for 45 minutes and then let the eggs cool in the vegetable water. Adding a bit of vinegar to the water makes the colors brighter. Polish the eggs with a soft cloth and some oil.

For 1 quart of water, use 6 tablespoons of onion skins, 4 cups of thistle leaves or spinach, or 1 cup of red beet juice.

Here are some old-fashioned Easter egg designs.

You can glue flowers and leaves on your eggs.

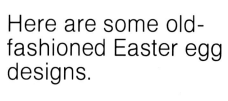

Sun

Life

Fertility

Dip your finger into paint and use it to make a design on the eggs.

Wrap the string around the egg in a design before dipping it into the dye. When you remove the string, you will find that you've made an interesting design.

Color and decorate some of the eggs with felt-tip markers.

Ottie, the Easter Hen

You will need:

Newspaper, papier-mâché paste, 1 balloon, plastic bowl, white paint, brush, colored paper, heavy white paper, scissors, glue, a few feathers, many eggs for the filling—chocolate candy eggs or hard-boiled eggs

1. Mix papier-mâché paste in the plastic bowl, following the directions on the package.

2. Blow up the balloon and knot the opening.

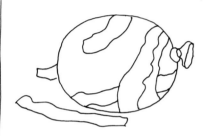

3. Tear newspaper into strips. Cover the strips with paste and wrap them around the balloon. Make several layers of newspaper strips.

4. Let the wrapped balloon dry for two days.

5. Cut a head and neck out of heavy white paper. Cut a beak and a crest out of colored paper and glue them to the head.

I'll make another one.

Glue head into slit.

6. Cut a hole in the hen's back. Make a slit for the head.

Paint the body of the hen white. Glue on the feathers. Now you can fill the Easter hen with eggs!

Glue on tail feathers, which are cut out of colored paper.

Here are some old-fashioned Easter egg designs.

You can glue flowers and leaves on your eggs.

Sun

Life

Fertility

Dip your finger into paint and use it to make a design on the eggs.

Wrap the string around the egg in a design before dipping it into the dye. When you remove the string, you will find that you've made an interesting design.

Color and decorate some of the eggs with felt-tip markers.

Ottie, the Easter Hen

You will need:

Newspaper, papier-mâché paste, 1 balloon, plastic bowl, white paint, brush, colored paper, heavy white paper, scissors, glue, a few feathers, many eggs for the filling—chocolate candy eggs or hard-boiled eggs

1. Mix papier-mâché paste in the plastic bowl, following the directions on the package.

2. Blow up the balloon and knot the opening.

3. Tear newspaper into strips. Cover the strips with paste and wrap them around the balloon. Make several layers of newspaper strips.

4. Let the wrapped balloon dry for two days.

5. Cut a head and neck out of heavy white paper. Cut a beak and a crest out of colored paper and glue them to the head.

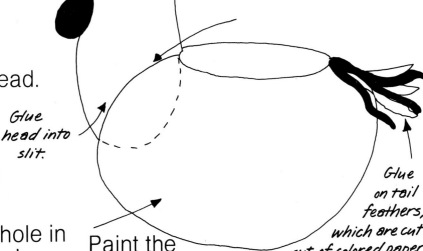

Glue head into slit.

Glue on tail feathers, which are cut out of colored paper.

I'll make another one.

6. Cut a hole in the hen's back. Make a slit for the head.

Paint the body of the hen white. Glue on the feathers. Now you can fill the Easter hen with eggs!

The Princess and the Rocking Dwarfs

You will need:

8 eggs, 1 cardboard tube from a toilet-paper roll, black yarn, glue, cotton batting, paints and brushes, scissors, small stones, crepe paper, large needle

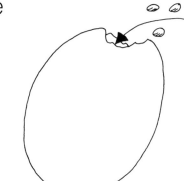

Dribble some glue in this hole and then drop some little stones on the glue.

1. Poke a ½-inch hole in each of the eggs with a large needle. Empty the eggs into a bowl. Wash out the shells.

2. Shake the little stones back and forth until the egg stands by itself.

Cotton-batting beard

3. Paint faces and clothes on the eggs.

4. Cut a hat out of crepe paper for each dwarf:

Glue

Roll up

Roll ¾ circle of paper into a pointed hat and glue the edges together.

If I push the dwarfs with my fingers, they rock!

Princess

Glue an eggshell on top of the cardboard tube. Paint a face on the eggshell.

Glue black yarn on the shell for hair. Cut a dress out of crepe paper.

Let the dwarfs rock on a level surface.

Small golden crown

Clay Egg Cup

If you want to use these egg cups for Easter, you have to make them two weeks ahead!

You will need:

Clay, a little bowl of water, a teaspoon, hard-boiled eggs, toothpick

1. Take a piece of clay and flatten it with your hand until all the air is out of it.

2. Shape the clay into a ball.

3. Use the spoon to hollow out a place to put the egg.

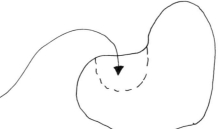

4. To make a bunny head: Take clay in your fingers, wet the clay with a bit of water from the bowl, and shape the head. Make clay arms.

5. With slip, wet the edges where the bunny's arms and head will be attached. (Make a slip by adding water to the clay and stirring until you have a paste.)

6. Use the toothpick to make holes for eyes and to scratch in a mouth and some whiskers.

7. The finished figures should dry for 2 weeks. Then they can be fired in a kiln.

   (CAUTION: Do not try to use a kiln yourself. Have an adult do the firing for you.)

   You can make other clay things for Easter, such as an egg cup in the shape of a chicken.

Egg Ducks

You will need:

One large needle, glue, some cardboard, scissors, pencil, 1 candle, matches, blown-out egg, waterproof paints, brushes

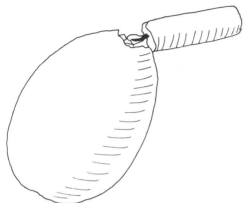

1. Burn a candle and let some wax drip into the blown-out egg.
   (CAUTION: Be careful! An adult should be present when you are using the candle. Or have an adult drip the wax for you.)

2. Close the egg openings with candle wax while the wax is still warm and you can shape it.

3. Let the egg swim in a bowl of water, and mark the place where you will put the head.

4. Cut a duck head out of cardboard. Cut line A up to the dotted line shown in the picture.

Bend backward.

a

Bend forward.

Now swim!

5. Glue the head to the egg and paint the duck with waterproof colors.

If you have a feather, glue it to the tail end of the duck.

44

Hopping Bunny—A Bunny Game for Two

<u>You will need:</u>

3 egg cartons, paints, brushes, scissors, clear tape, 5 little wooden sticks, construction paper, yarn or string, 30 corks, glue, 2 plastic forks

1. Cut the tops and front flaps off the egg cartons. Cut one carton in half the long way. Tape a 6-egg carton and the two 12-egg cartons all together so that you have one 30-egg carton. Divide the big carton into five parts and paint each part a different color. (See photo on opposite page.)

2. Cut off two little "hats" from one of the egg-carton tops. Paint the hats yellow.

These are yellow in the picture.

Cut the lower edge evenly.

3. Cut flags from construction paper and glue them to the wooden sticks. Number them 10, 20, 30, 40, and 50. Put a flag in each color area of the carton.

4. Every player has fifteen cork bunnies. To make the two sides different, give one set white ears and one set yellow ears.

When the game is made, put it on a level surface to play.

Paint eyes on.

Make whiskers from yarn or string.

How to play the game:

Put a yellow hat on the end of a fork handle. Press the prongs of the fork and try to flip the hat into one of the sections of the egg carton. Put one of your little bunnies into each hole that you hit. Players take turns flipping the hat. When all the holes are filled with bunnies, count up your points. (Use the number on the flag for that section.)

Hurray, it flies!

Bunny, Bunny, Easter Bunny

You will need:

Newspapers, papier-mâché paste, paint, crepe paper, glue, bowl, water, 1 wooden stick

1. Cover the work area with newspapers. Crush a lot of newspaper into a big ball for the body.

2. Make a smaller ball of crushed paper for the head.

To hold crushed newspaper, wrap it several times with tape.

3. Mix papier-mâché paste in the bowl, following the directions on the package.

4. Let the mixed paste stand for ten minutes before mixing it again thoroughly.

5. Tear newspaper into long strips.

6. Wet the strips with paste and wrap them around the paper ball. Repeat this several times.

What can I put into the bunny?

7. Form two long ears and wet them with paste.

8. Let everything dry for two or three days.

9. Glue the dry pieces together and paint them.

10. You may leave the bunny as it is now, or cut a hole in the bottom, take out some of the extra paper, and put a little present into the hole.

Egg Games

Here are some games with hard-boiled eggs. Would you like to play them with your friends?

I give you an egg. If you break it, you'll have two.

Oh! Someone lost an egg.

Egg Race

You probably know about racing with eggs. Players put an egg on a spoon and run with it around a special course.

Egg Thief

Put strings around eggs and put them in the middle of a table. Each player holds on to his or her egg. One player tries to capture an egg by putting the bowl over it while telling stories or jokes to divert the other player's attention. Players must be attentive and pull their eggs away. Whoever keeps the egg the longest time can be "egg thief" for the next turn.

Put eggs in the middle.

50

Egg Rolling

The players let their eggs roll down a hill or down a slanted board. Which egg will roll the fastest?

Egg Marbles

Draw a circle on the ground. Five players put their eggs in the circle. The sixth player rolls an egg into the circle. If the egg hits one of the eggs in the circle, the owner has to give the egg to the sixth player. The player who ends up with the most eggs wins.

Egg Throwing

Every player gets an equal number of eggs. The eggs will be thrown into a swaying basket! Whose aim is the best?

Juggler

You will need:

6 blown-out eggs, wire, cardboard, paints and brushes, scissors

1. Paint the eggs different colors. Let them dry and thread them onto a wire. Double or triple the wire strand to make the wire stronger.

Use the wire double or even triple.

Cut holes.

2. Cut a bunny from sturdy cardboard. You also need a strip of cardboard.

The striped end will be covered with glue and stuck to the back of the bunny so that he can stand up.

3. Bend the wire that holds the eggs to form a wreath of eggs. Put the ends of the wire through holes A and B. Knot the ends of the wire behind the bunny's head.

Now the bunny can stand on the lawn or at the breakfast table.

Easter Pyramid

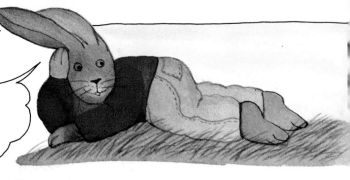

This Easter pyramid has little egg figures hanging on it—one for each month of the year.

You will need:

1 long and 3 shorter lengths of wooden lath, hammer, nail, flower wire, crepe paper, 12 blown-out eggs, paints and brushes, wooden sticks, a cork, matchsticks, string, thread, 1 flowerpot with soil

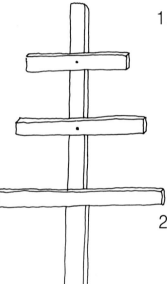

1. Nail the laths together as you see here.
    (CAUTION: Be careful with the hammer and nails.
    Or have an adult do the hammering for you.)

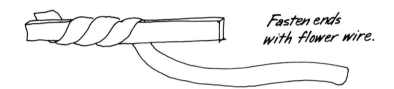

Fasten ends with flower wire.

2. Stick the wooden framework into the soil in the flowerpot.
    Wrap the framework with crepe paper.

Hold on here and turn.

3. Now paint the blown-out eggs. It's easy to do when you put the egg on a stick that is pushed into a cork.

Paint an egg for every month of the year. For January, a snowman; for February, a heart; and so on.

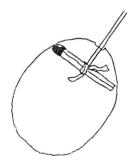

To hang the eggs

Tie thread around the middle of a piece of matchstick. Push the stick into the larger hole in the egg. The matchstick will turn sideways in the egg and secure the thread.

Hen and Chicks

You will need:

1 roll yellow crepe paper, red construction paper, glue, scissors, 1 blown-out egg, straight pins with black heads, small candy eggs

1. Cut the crepe paper roll into strips. It might not be easy. Ask an adult to help you.

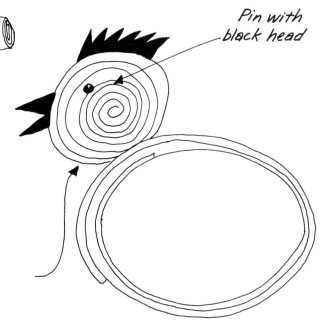

Pin with black head

2. To make the hen: Wrap the egg with crepe paper. Glue the first part as you wrap. Between each few rounds, put on some drops of glue. The head is made from rolled crepe paper and glued to the body. Cut a beak and a comb from red construction paper and glue them on.

I'll glue some feathers on for the tail.

The chicks are made of rolled paper, too, but they have no egg in the middle. Glue on red beaks.

You can also make bunnies out of brown paper, using the same method.

Put the finished animals on a table or outside.

A Nest Full of Mice

You will need:

Hard-boiled or blown-out eggs, paper, straight pins with black heads (or small black beads), scissors, glue, some yarn or straw for the nest

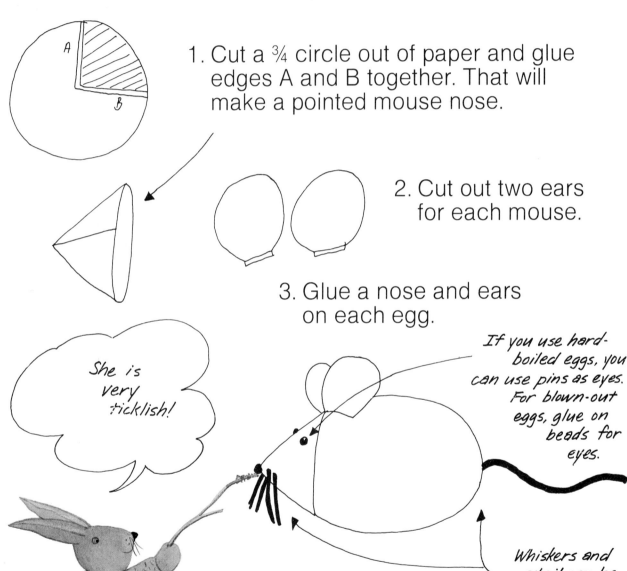

1. Cut a ¾ circle out of paper and glue edges A and B together. That will make a pointed mouse nose.

2. Cut out two ears for each mouse.

3. Glue a nose and ears on each egg.

She is very ticklish!

If you use hard-boiled eggs, you can use pins as eyes. For blown-out eggs, glue on beads for eyes.

Whiskers and a tail can be made from yarn and glued on.

You can paint the mice or leave them white. Set the mice in a nest of yarn or straw.

Bunny House

You will need:

A round box, 1 blown-out egg, some moss and flowers, colored paper, scissors, paints, cotton batting, glue, a few colored candy eggs

1. Cut out ¾ circle from red paper and glue edges A and B together. This is the roof.

2. Glue the roof to the top of the egg.

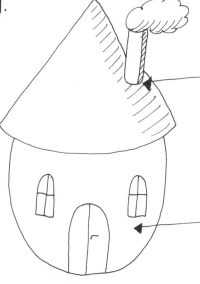

Cut a hole in the roof for the chimney. Make the chimney from rolled-up paper. Glue it on. Glue on a puff of cotton for smoke.

Cut doors and windows out of colored paper, and glue them on.

3. Put moss into the box with the house.

He loves me, he loves me not...

Paint the box.

Cut a door.

60

Bunny Hand Puppet

This is too difficult for you to knit, but maybe an aunt or your mother will knit it!

You will need:

A skein of soft white yarn; 1 set (4) of double-pointed knitting needles, size 7; 2 small, dark buttons; cotton batting for filling

Body and Head:

Cast on 28 sts. (7 per needle) and purl 2 rows. Knit from now on. Knit 4 rows and in the 5th row, increase 4 sts. (1 st. on each needle). Knit 4 rows and increase again in the 5th. Repeat once more until there are 40 sts. Knit 2 rows and in the 3rd row knit 2 sts. together, once on each needle. Knit 2 rows and decrease again in the 3rd row until 32 sts. are left. Then knit 10 rows. On the 11th row, first needle, knit 2 sts., cast off 4 sts., knit 2 sts. Do the same on 2nd needle. Finish row by knitting on needles 3 and 4.

In the 12th row cast on over the 4 sts. that were cast off in the previous row (these holes are for the paws). Now knit another 10 rows. In the 11th, make holes for the ears by knitting needles 1 and 2, then on the 3rd needle, knit 2 sts., cast off 4 sts., knit 2 sts. Repeat on 4th needle. 12th row: Again cast on 4 sts. where sts. were cast off. Knit 4 rows and in the 5th row increase 4 sts. (1 on each needle). Knit 6 rows (there should be 9 sts. on each of the 4 needles). In the next row knit 2 sts. together at beginning of each needle. In the following row, knit 2 sts. together at the end of each needle. Repeat these last 2 rows.

Cut the yarn, thread the end through the remaining 20 sts., drawing them together. Finish off the ends.

Paws:

Cast on 12 sts. from one of the body paw-holes, divided evenly onto 3 needles. Knit 5 rows. In 6th row knit 2 sts., knit 3rd and 4th sts. together, and repeat twice (9 sts. remain). Knit 9 rows, cut yarn, pull end through all 9 sts., pulling them together, and finish off. Repeat for other paw.

Ears:

Each ear is knitted in 2 parts, using only 2 needles, knitting 1 row and purling the next. It may be easier to make ears and sew them on.

Inner ear:

Cast on 9 sts., knit (and purl) 12 rows. 13th row, decrease 1 st. at beginning and end of row. Knit 4 rows. In 5th row, again decrease 2 sts. Knit 3 rows, in 4th row decrease 2 sts. Knit 5 rows, cut yarn and draw the last 3 sts. together. Finish off.

Outer Ear:

The same as inner ear, only begin with 11 sts. Sew two parts together, stuff cotton batting into ears.

Stuff head and paws, sew on 2 buttons for eyes, add different-colored yarn for nose. That's it!

INDEX